stolen
verses
and
other
poems

A BILINGUAL EDITION

Northwestern University Press
Evanston, Illinois

stolen verses and other poems

OSCAR HAHN

Translated from the Spanish
and with an introduction
by James Hoggard

Hydra Books
Northwestern University Press
Evanston, Illinois 60208-4210

These poems were originally published in Spanish in *Estrellas fijas en un cielo blanco* (Santiago de Chile: Editorial Universitaria, 1989), *Versos robados* (Madrid: Visor, 1995), and *Antología virtual* (Santiago de Chile: Fondo de Cultura Económica, 1996). Copyright © by Oscar Hahn. Hydra Books/Northwestern University Press edition published 2000 by arrangement with Oscar Hahn.

Grateful acknowledgment is made to the following publications in which many of these translations first appeared, some in forms slightly different from those here: *Americas Review; ACM; Clackamas Literary Review; Exchanges; Manoa; Mississippi Review; Mr. Knife, Miss Fork; Piedmont Literary Review; Two Lines;* and *Xavier Review.*

Printed in the United States of America

ISBN 0-8101-1778-9

Library of Congress Cataloging-in-Publication Data

Hahn, Oscar, 1938–
  Stolen verses and other poems / Oscar Hahn ; translated from the Spanish with an introduction by James Hoggard.
    p. cm.
  English and Spanish.
  ISBN 0-8101-1778-9 (hc.)
    I. Hoggard, James. II. Title.

PQ8097.H26 A24 2000
861—dc21

99-088366

The paper used in this publication meets the minimum requirements of the American National Standard for Information Sciences—Permanence of Paper for Printed Library Materials, ANSI Z39.48-1984.

Todos mis versos son ajenos
Yo tal vez los robé

All my verses are somebody else's
Maybe I stole them

Contents

Translator's Acknowledgments

I would like to thank several people who, through the years, have made suggestions and responded to questions I had about sound, rhythm, and meaning. I appreciate their generosity of attention: Linda Hollabaugh, Julie Dunkelberg, Adalberto García, Roberto Fuertes-Manjón, Addie Ebner, and always, day and night, Lynn Hoggard.

Books by Oscar Hahn

Esta rosa negra, 1961

Agua final, 1967

Arte de morir, 1977 (*The Art of Dying,* 1988)

Mal de amor, 1981 (*Love Breaks,* 1991)

Imágenes nucleares, 1983

*Texto sobre texto: Aproximaciones a Herrera y
      Reissig, Borges, Cortázar, Huidobro, Lihn,* 1984

Flor de enamorados, 1987

Estrellas fijas en un cielo blanco, 1989

Poemas selectos, 1989

Tratado de sortilegios, 1992

Versos robados, 1995

Antología virtual, 1996

Antología retroactiva, 1998

Born in Chile in 1938, Oscar Hahn has become an increasingly important figure in Spanish American poetry over the last twenty years. When his first sizable volume, *Arte de morir* (*The Art of Dying*), was published in Buenos Aires in 1977, Hahn was hailed by one of the masters of postmodernism in Chile, Enrique Lihn, as "the premier poet of his generation." In a lengthy review of the same work, the critic Graciela Palau de Nemes called Hahn "the most important poet of the fantastic in Spanish American letters." Even earlier Pablo Neruda had praised Hahn for his "great originality and intensity," and Mario Vargas Llosa, one of the most highly respected writers of our time, has called Hahn's work "magnificent and truly original . . . the most personal I've read in the poetry of our language in a long time." These notable figures were responding to a poet with a cosmopolitan sensibility and an unusual ability to write authentically in numerous styles.

Whether writing sonnets, ballads, or free verse, Hahn has his own voice, one that moves artfully between coolly focused, often witty observation and intense, apocalyptic energy. What connects the disparate styles is a commanding, even infectious articulation of strangeness in the world. Some of the poems evoke lovely, gracefully phrased whispers; others have rhythms and attitudes that seem nightmarishly rough. Some are political in import, some droll, others wild with rage. But the world has always been complex, and Hahn is not the first artist to feel at home with the horrors of darkness and the sweetness of light. Cervantes and Dante, Shakespeare and Sophocles, Mozart and Goya, Beethoven and van Gogh: we go to these figures to experience the world with powerful clarity. We might also recall a single moment in a Spanish prison when, thinking of his beloved Josefina, the deathly ill poet Miguel Hernández wrote, "Yo no quiero más luz que tu cuerpo ante el mío [I want no more light than your body before mine]."

Like his early poems, Hahn's later work is distinctive in that it appears simultaneously direct and oblique. The reason is that Hahn's poetry is most often dramatic. His speakers seem in turn lyrical, troubled, sly, reflective, or even splendidly unhinged. The implications of the works are nevertheless clear because, however complex the poems are, Hahn's sensibility remains coherent. The dramatic quality draws together both personal and universal dimensions of the poetry, which is what a lively sense of mythos has always been able to do. Some of the speakers, as in this volume, are historical figures, cultural icons that name notable points of reference: Friedrich Nietzsche at a sanatorium in Basel, Sigmund Freud under hypnosis, Juan Rulfo dying, John Lennon talking with death. Others, especially those in a number of the sonnets from *Estrellas fijas en un cielo blanco* (*Fixed Stars in a White Sky*) reflect on artistic or sacramental concerns. Whether uttering a prayerful appeal, as in "Read My Defective Verses Lord," or contemplating Fra Angelico's painting *The Annunciation,* or seeing domestic strife as a truncated sonnet, or answering the question "Why do you write?" Hahn's speakers often consider form itself a prominent dimension of subject matter. The reason for that seems clear. Integrity of form modifies the terrors of experience, and the poems refer to many points of separation and breakage.

The presentation of the Adam-and-Eve-in-Eden myth in "Triptych" is especially effective in showing Hahn's obliqueness of approach. The speaker in the guise of Adam sounds more like a meditative contemporary than a figure in an ancient story from what's now called the Middle East. The triptych begins with an elegant intimation of a common problem in modernism and postmodernism—the unreachableness of certainty:

> *I opened the seven doors of desire*
> *and discovered I wanted nothing there:*
> *I've sought the speech of the ineffable*
> *but its sounds are incomprehensible*

Then in the third poem in the sequence, "Expulsion from Paradise," he begins by addressing his mate with lyrical sensuosity that contains reminders of the mysterious, compensatory wonders there are in intimacy:

Your bed, the garden of delights
your body, three graces flesht
your fruits and flowers caressing me,
intimately you empty me

. . . .

Roaming the edges of dark heights
we celebrate demonic rites
in bedrooms whose beds are on fire

And when we flee those wicked spells
a winged being with lily afire
waits for us at the door of desire

A more immediate sense of harshness is found in "Old Year 1973," which evokes the speaker's bitter sense of helplessness in a midnight toast in which the overthrow and murder of the duly elected Salvador Allende are remembered. Hahn himself had been a strong supporter of Allende, and after the horror of the assassination and the rise of Augusto Pinochet to power, Hahn was thrown, uncharged, into prison and threatened repeatedly with execution. The bloodiness of political upheaval is also evoked in the elegiac, keenly structured "A Pensive Drowned Man Sometimes Drifts." This poem, like a number of his others, has a litany-like dimension and echoic effects in its phrasing, as in the closing lines, which allude to one of the wonders of Jesus:

Holding hands the corpses go:
walking on the water in silence

The periodically allusive quality of Hahn's verse keeps one connected to the grandness of tradition. As a result, contemporary matters are seen in historical perspective. At the same time, past events can be read as metaphors of contemporary situations, as is the case in *Arte de morir* with one of Hahn's most powerful poems, "Vision of Hiroshima." The description of the immediate effects of the atomic bombing of a Japanese city in 1945 can be read as an indirect reference to the horrible violence engendered by various kinds of tyrants and their characteristic attitude of cruel indifference to the concerns of others. In this poem and in ritualistic proclamations such as "Litany for a Dead Poet," Hahn assumes the mantle of the prophet, the one who speaks out in defense of the fine and in condemnation of the unjust. Thoroughly controlled yet heartbreaking in its impact, "To a Santiago Washerwoman" shows the horrors of violent torture at a personal level:

> *My cousin who lived off her tubs*
> *suddenly died on me:*
> *one blow from a rifle butt*
> *and her head opened up*
>
> *Out of her splayed skull's pit*
> *screams and fraternal songs rise*

Even in such a poem, though, Hahn embraces the perspective provided by a mythic frame of reference:

> *A regiment of stained men passes:*
> *so dirty even Purgatory's purger*
> *could never clean their uniforms*

He gives voice to what many who lack his access to the fantastic might call unspeakable.

Perhaps as much as anything else it's the inclusive quality of Hahn's sensibility, his versatility in idea and form, that distinguishes him from so many other contemporary poets. Believable in his poetic gestures of keenly focused sobriety and in the quality of restraint that often makes tensions in his work seem explosive, he is also effective when he turns whimsical mid dark turns of mind. A good example is found in the wickedly imaginative depiction of the battle between the sexes in "Praying Mantis":

> *Hey they'll eat up a guy*
> *They'll eat him with the upper hole*
> *and with the lower hole*
>
> *Laughing with their little polyhedral eyes*
> *my school buddies*
> *called me Fly*

In "Heartbreak Hotel" he is even able to bring together, into one complex, groups as disparate as idly rebellious rock-and-roll devotees of the 1950s and recent political victims. Here, too, wit emerges as a force of perception that is indicative of power and imagination. That's not surprising, though, from one who can turn droll enough to give us a poem titled "At the Nudist Beach of the Unconscious."

Quite often in contemporary literature and its peripatetic cousin pop culture, surrealism has been considered synonymous with the weird or bizarre. Throughout its European flowering in the 1920s and 1930s, a period that drew a number of South American poets to its chimeras, these elements were certainly present. But the driving aim of surrealism, however whimsical its effects might have sometimes seemed, was not merely to divert but also to articulate the presence of realms beyond the phenomenal. A form of romanticism, it embraced the marvelous in order to guide one simultaneously inward toward the primal elements behind self and outward toward the transcendent.

Appropriately enough, it's in surrealism that one tends to find twentieth-century love poems, an idiom that seems curiously scarce elsewhere. The reason is obvious: In surrealism we have an approach to experience and art in which the sacredness of connection between self and other is taken seriously. Eros is seen as the function of relationship, an affirmation of the spiritual possibilities of bodily beings. This attitude is something quite different from the self-referential character of libidinous pursuit or the cool (or even hot) observations of social study. Surveying the range of Hahn's work while recognizing the notable presence of the fantastic in it, one is not surprised to find a sizable variety of love poems. In fact, his second major book, *Mal de amor* (*Love Breaks*), is a collection of love poems. The beloved is absent from the speaker, however, except in memory; but in certain respects that's appropriate because the poems focus on the strange limits of connection between self and other, the other in this case being the idea of place as well as the fact of another person. Oddly enough, the book was banned by the Pinochet junta soon after it was published; no reason was given. Then five years later the book was republished in an expanded edition. In 1989 a collection of essays on Hahn's work was published as *Asedios a Oscar Hahn* (*Approaches to Oscar Hahn*), and a number of awards followed.

Stolen Verses and Other Poems brings together the poems in Hahn's latest single collection, *Versos robados* (*Stolen Verses*), with a gathering of sonnets from *Estrellas fijas en un cielo blanco* and other poems that have not appeared in previous collections of translations I have published of his work. One sees in this volume the stylistic and conceptual ranges that have characterized his verse. At the same time there is a liveliness of spirit that conveys the freshness of his vision. In many respects Hahn has not been a terrifically prolific poet; he's been a careful poet, one who has insisted that his poems sing before he lets them go. For this reason they let us experience vividly the complex turns of his world. His voice is his own, but that voice also carries with it echoes from tradition. Self is seen in the context of the other, while the other, full of stories, conveys interesting inventions of self.

A Note on the Translation

Respecting the verse forms used by a poet encourages a translator to think about parallels and differences in sound and rhythm among languages. This is especially true when working with sonnets. Two notable differences between Spanish and English seem immediately obvious: Spanish is a much more rhyme-rich language than English, and Spanish phrases often have more syllables than their English equivalents. As a result, I chose to use a four-beat line in the translations of most of the sonnets in the "Fixed Stars in a White Sky" section; in "Why Do You Write?" however, I followed Hahn's example of using a longer line and employed a six-beat line throughout the poem. In regard to rhyme, I kept in mind the alliterative heritage of English and often relied on sonic effects such as assonance, consonance, and alliteration—in the sonnets as well as the other poems—to evoke elements of musicality found in the originals. Paying attention to the fluidity of the poems in Spanish, I employed liquids and sibilants prominently, particularly in the sonnets where numerous rhymes and half-rhymes are used, often for closure but also to intensify echoic effects. Hahn does not let himself be hypnotized by the metronome. Accepting that element of variety as a model, and not wanting the translations to sound affected, I kept the idea of equivalence more vividly in mind than mirrorlike doubling.

stolen
verses
and
other
poems

versos robados

stolen verses

Meditación al atardecer

¿En qué piensa la última rosa del verano
mientras ve desfallecer su color
y evaporarse su perfume?

¿En qué piensa la última nieve del invierno
mientras mira esos rayos de sol
que se abren paso entre las nubes?

¿Y en qué piensa ese hombre
a la hora del crepúsculo
sentado en una roca frente al mar?

En la última rosa del verano
En la última nieve del invierno

Meditation at Dusk

What does summer's last rose think about
as it sees its color fading
and its fragrance vanishing?

What does winter's last snow think about
as it looks at those sunrays
that force their way through the clouds?

And what does that man think about
at twilight
sitting on a rock by the sea?

About summer's last rose
About winter's last snow

Higiene bucal

Tomo una escobilla de dientes
y la mojo con agua bendita

La escobilla comienza a arder
como trapo empapado en gasolina

Las cerdas arden y arden
junto a la llave de agua profana

Tomo la escobilla en llamas
y me lavo los dientes uno a uno

Si a la escobilla se le ocurre apagarse
todos nos apagaremos de súbito

Rezo porque se quede encendida
y libere de pecados mi verbo

Podré sonreírle al Altísimo
con la boca llena de cenizas

Oral Hygiene

I take a toothbrush
and wet it with holy water

Like a rag soaked in gasoline
the brush begins to burn

The bristles burn on and on
near the profane water tap

I take the flaming brush
and one by one I clean my teeth

If the fire on the brush burns out
we'll suddenly all burn out

I pray it keeps on burning
and frees my speech from sin

With my mouth full of ashes I'll
be able to smile at the Almighty

Una noche en el Café Berlioz

Yo he visto su cara en otra parte le dije
cuando entró en el Café Berlioz

Soy de otra dimensión contestó sonriendo
y avanzó hacia el fondo del salón

Ella finje escribir en su mesa de mármol
pero me observa de reojo

Desde mi mesa veo su cuello desnudo

Como un aerolito cruzó mi mente
el rostro de Muriel mi amante muerta

Usted es zurda le dije acercándome
Hacemos la pareja perfecta

Tomé su lápiz y escribí "te amo"
con mi mano derecha en la servilleta

Rey del lugar común respondió sin mirarme
mientras le echaba azúcar al té

Me ha clavado una estaca en el corazón
Me ha lanzado una bala de plata
Me ha ahorcado con una trenza de ajo

Volví confundido a mi mesa
con la cola de diablo entre las piernas

En este punto las sombras de los clientes
pagaron y se fueron del Café Berlioz

Váyanse espíritus les dije furioso
agitando mi paraguas chamuscado

¿Hay alguna Muriel aquí?
gritó la mesera desde el umbral

One Night at the Berlioz Café

When she entered the Berlioz Café
I said I've seen your face somewhere

I'm from another dimension she answered smiling
and went on toward the back of the lounge

She acts as if she's writing on the marble tabletop
but she's watching me out of the corner of her eye

From my table I see her bare neck

Like a meteor the face of Muriel
my dead lover crossed my mind

You're left-handed I said walking nearer
We make the perfect couple

I took her pencil and with my right hand
wrote "I love you" on the napkin

King of the common place she replied not looking at me
as she poured sugar in her tea

She drove a stake in my heart
She shot me with a silver bullet
She hanged me with a string of garlic

I went back to my table confused
the devil's tail between my legs

At that point the customers' shadows
paid up and left the Berlioz Café

Get out spirits I yelled at them
shaking my singed umbrella

Is there a Muriel here?
the waitress called from the doorway

Cuando ella caminó hacia la puerta
vi que tenía una cruz en la mano

Por favor tráiganme la cuenta
que ya está por salir el sol

La lluvia penetra por los agujeros de mi memoria

Muriel Muriel
¿por qué me has abandonado?

When she walked toward the door
I saw she had a cross in her hand

Please bring me the bill
because the sun's already rising

Rain leaks through the holes in my memory

Muriel Muriel
why have you left me?

Lapidario

Mostrada sea la naturaleza de las piedras
y la fuerza que reciben de las estrellas

Mostradas sean sus virtudes y poderes
y sus formas y sus brillos y sus signos

La piedra llamada congelamiento
se aloja donde están los hondos miedos

Si el sujeto la ve abre ojos y boca
y no vuelve a cerrarlos nunca más

Pero si sobre ella se posa la tórtola en llamas
se le acaba el poder para siempre

A la piedra que dicen de la abstinencia
ni siquiera el diamante puede romperla

Cuando brilla engastada en el dedo
ahuyenta a las bestias lascivas

Su cuerpo es caliente y húmedo
y su color aúlla en la noche

A la piedra nombrada del sueño
ni aun el odio puede hacerle daño

Durante el día se asoma por el oído
De noche es clara semejante al fuego

El que la carga en el pecho se queda dormido
y no despierta hasta que se la quitan

A veces es llamada piedra de la muerte

Por último hay también la piedra de la locura
que se halla donde está la gran tiniebla

Lapidary

Let the nature of the rocks be shown
and the power they receive from the stars

Let their virtues and strengths be shown
and their forms and brightness and signs

The rock called frostbite
is lodged where the deep fears are

If the subject sees it he opens his eyes and mouth
and never closes them again

But if the flaming dove lights on it
its power is gone forever

As far as the rock called abstinence goes
not even the diamond can break it

When it shines set on the finger
it scares off lewd beasts

Its body is warm and moist
and at night its color howls

As far as the rock named dream goes
not even hatred can harm it

During the day it sticks out of the ear
By night it's bright like fire

Whoever has it on his chest falls asleep
and doesn't wake up till he's rid of it

Sometimes it's called the rock of death

Finally there's the rock of madness
that's found where the great darkness is

Sana al endemoniado que se la ata al cuello
y camina en el aire cuando sale la luna

Si la mueles y mezclas con el agua del mar
podrás untar tu pluma y escribir tu epitafio

A-E-I-O-U
para que salgas tú
y la lleves tú

It heals the demon-mad one who ties it around his neck
and walks on air when the moon appears

If you grind it and mix it with seawater
you can ink your pen and write your epitaph

Eeny meeny miny moe
catch a tiger
by the toe

La mantis religiosa

Sobre todo la Mantis
Cualquier tipo de insecto
pero sobre todo la Mantis

Quizás su montón de muslos
o su montón de ojos
o las dos cosas juntas

Se comen al macho fíjate
Se lo comen por el agujero de arriba
y por el de abajo

El Mosco me llamaban
mis compañeros de colegio
riéndose con sus ojitos poliédricos

La Mantis secreta una oscura saliva
que ciega a los incautos

¿Por qué me abrazas oye?
¿Por qué me clavas tus uñas en la espalda?

Me extraña araña le dije

Te conozco Mosco dijo la loca
limpiándose la sangre de las uñas

La religiosidad de la Mantis
no puede ponerse en duda: me refiero
a la Última Cena me dijo saboreándome

El peso de las pesadillas

El peso de las pesadillas
en el cerebro de los vivientes

Praying Mantis

Especially the Mantis
Any type of insect
but especially the Mantis

Perhaps it's their heap of thighs
or their heap of eyes
or the two of them together

Hey they'll eat up a guy
They'll eat him with the upper hole
and with the lower hole

Laughing with their little polyhedral eyes
my school buddies
called me Fly

The Mantis secretes a dark spit
that'll blind a careless guy

Hey why're you hugging me?
Digging your nails in my back?

Lady you're messing my mind

I know you Fly crazy lady replied
cleaning her bloody fingernails

The piety of the Mantis
can't be denied: I mean
the Last Supper she said savoring me

The weight of nightmares

The weight of nightmares
in the minds of those still alive

Nietzsche en el sanatorio de Basilea

Esta calle que baja dura una eternidad

Aquí se cuecen vivos los grandes pensamientos

Ha llegado la hora del descanso en que no se descansa
Cuando los perros creen en santas y en fantasmas

En este punto mi madre y mi hermana preguntaron sin voz
¿Y qué sabes tú de todo eso?

Me han enterrado dos veces este otoño mamá

De repente el huracán me separó las alas con violencia
y el ataúd se rompió

¿Qué hace mi hermana en el bosque?
Su fantasma salió de mis propias cenizas

Mi espada quiere beber de su sangre
y centellea con ardiente deseo

Mi madre es un viento que seca los árboles frutales

Y qué sabes tú de todo eso preguntaron sin voz

Los niños y las amapolas son inocentes
hasta en su maldad recitaron en coro

Ahora oigo sonar sus viejas caras
Las de mi madre y las de mi hermana

La tierra tiene piel y esa piel padece enfermedades
replicaron llorando

Es cierto hijo que eres una noche de oscuras risas

¿De dónde sacas lo que vomitas?
Sal de tus profundidades oye

Nietzsche in the Sanatorium at Basel

This street keeps going down forever

Great thoughts are boiled alive here

Rest time has come when there is no rest
When dogs believe in saints and ghosts

Then my mother and my sister voicelessly asked
And what do you know about all that?

Mama they've buried me twice this fall

Suddenly the hurricane ripped my wings off
and the casket broke

What's my sister doing in the woods?
Her ghost emerged from my own ashes

My sword wants to drink your blood
it's scintillant with hot desire

My mother's a wind that scorches the fruit trees

And what do you know about all that they voicelessly asked

Children and poppies are innocent
even when they're evil they recited in chorus

Now I hear their old faces moaning
My mother's and my sister's

The earth has a skin and that skin gets sick
they replied crying

Son you really are a night of dark laughs

Where do you get what you vomit?
Hey come on out of your profundities

Ahora el sol me derrite y los perros me lamen la piel

Eres un charco de muerte en las pesadillas
de los condenados al sueño me gritaron las brujas

Soy un charco de sueño en las pesadillas
de los condenados a muerte queridas

En este punto volvieron a decirme sin voz
¿Y qué sabes tú de todo eso?

Váyanse al mismo diablo les dije

Esta calle que baja
no acaba nunca de bajar

Now the sun melts me and dogs lick my skin

You're a puddle of death in the nightmares
of those condemned to dream the witches screamed

I'm a puddle of dreams dears
in the nightmares of those condemned to death

Then again they asked me voicelessly
And what do you know about all that?

Go to hell I told them

This street going down
never stops going down

Silla mecedora

Me duelen las piernas dijo la silla
Están llenas de várices

Siento unas gotas de sudor frío
bajando por mi respaldo

En vez de astillas tengo espinas
y mi asiento se cubre de llagas

No sé de dónde salió este hombre
que está sentado en mí sangrando

Al tercer día se puso de pie
y voló por la ventana del cuarto

Y el viento empezó a mecerme
como si nada hubiera pasado

Rocking Chair

My legs hurt the chair said
They're full of varicose veins

I feel drops of cold sweat
going down my back

Instead of splinters I have thorns
and my seat's covered with sores

This man who's sitting here bleeding on me
I don't know where he came from

On the third day he stood up
and flew out the apartment's window

And the wind began to rock me
as if nothing had happened

En una estación del Metro

Desventurados los que divisaron
a una muchacha en el Metro

y se enamoraron de golpe
y la siguieron enloquecidos

y la perdieron para siempre entre la multitud

Porque ellos serán condenados
a vagar sin rumbo por la estaciones

y a llorar con las canciones de amor
que los músicos ambulantes entonan en los túneles

Y quizás el amor no es más que eso:

una mujer o un hombre que desciende de un carro
en cualquier estación del Metro

y resplandece unos segundos
y se pierde en la noche sin nombre

In a Station of the Metro

Curst are those who saw
a girl in the Metro

and fell in love at first sight
and followed her madly

and lost her forever in the crowd

For they shall be condemned
to wander back and forth through the stations

and cry at the love songs
the itinerant musicians play in the tunnels

And maybe love's no more than that:

a woman or a man getting out of a car
in some station of the Metro

and shining a few seconds
and fading away in the nameless night

A las doce del día

Estaba tendido boca arriba en el parque
mirando el cielo azul esplendoroso

Sentía el frescor de la brisa
sobre mi rostro caliente por el sol

De pronto noté la inmovilidad absoluta de los árboles
Un gran silencio descendió sobre el paisaje

En la superficie del lago pero sin tocar el agua
aparecieron las esferas

Me senté apoyado contra un árbol para verlas mejor

Eran las doce del día
y de golpe empezó a anochecer

Las esferas estaban suspendidas sobre el agua fija
claramente visibles en la oscuridad

Una pista de aterrizaje se encendió a la distancia

Las esferas despegaron a toda velocidad
y de súbito estaban encima mío

No eran de metal sino de materia orgánica
Blancas con una circunferencia azul en el centro

Y me miraban fijamente

Después desde las esferas me vi a mí mismo
sentado en el pasto con las cuencas vacías

Me vi levantándome penosamente en la oscuridad

Me vi avanzando a tientas por el parque allá abajo
hasta que la Tierra fue un punto borroso en el cosmos

A las doce del día
Desde la constelación de Andrómeda

At Noon

I was lying face up in the park
looking at the glorious blue sky

I felt the coolness of the breeze
on my sunwarmed face

Suddenly I noticed the trees' absolute stillness
A great silence settled on the scene

Without touching the water
spheres appeared on the surface of the lake

I sat back against a tree to see them better

It was noon
and suddenly began to grow dark

Clearly visible in the darkness
the spheres were suspended on the still water

In the distance a landing strip was lighted up

The spheres took off at full speed
and were suddenly above me

They weren't metal but some organic material
White with a blue circle in the center

And they fixed their gaze on me

Later from the spheres I saw myself
sitting in the field with empty eyesockets

I saw myself standing up painfully in the darkness

I saw myself moving tentatively through the park down there
until the Earth became an indistinct dot in the cosmos

At noon
From the constellation Andromeda

Rulfo en la hora de su muerte

Había una luna grande en medio del mundo

Era vieja de muchos años y flaca
como si le hubieran estirado el cuero

Esta es mi muerte dijo
Si usted viera el gentío de ánimas
que andan sueltas por la calle

Estoy aquí boca arriba
pensando en aquel tiempo para borrar mi soledad

Me mataron los murmullos

Y se fue montado en su macho sin mirar hacia atrás
dejándonos la imagen de la perdición

Él duerme
No lo despierten
No hagan ruido

Duró varias horas luchando con sus pensamientos
Tirándolos al agua negra del río

Y se fue desmoronando
como un montón de piedras

Rulfo in the Hour of His Death

There was a big moon in the middle of the world

It was extremely old and skinny
as if its hide had been stretched

This he said is my death
If you had seen the throng of spirits
walking loose through the street

Here I am on my back
thinking about that time to erase my loneliness

The murmurs killed me

And he mounted up on his mule without looking back
leaving us the image of doom

He's asleep
Don't wake him up
Don't make any noise

He lasted several hours struggling with his thoughts
Throwing them into the river's black water

And he was wearing away
like a pile of stones

En la playa nudista del inconsciente

Un hombre está tendido en la playa nudista del inconsciente
a esa hora de la noche en que salen dos soles

La parte mujer del hombre corre graciosamente hacia el agua
La parte hombre camina en dirección a la orilla

En la playa nudista del inconsciente
las dos partes se bañan tomadas de la mano

El sol negro se alza en el horizonte
El sol blanco se pone al rojo vivo

La mujer y el hombre hacen el amor hasta el vértigo
Sus cuerpos luchan en la arena fosforescente

Y el firmamento se llena de aerolitos
que se desplazan a la velocidad de la luz

At the Nudist Beach of the Unconscious

A man is lying on the nudist beach of the unconscious
at that time of night when two suns appear

The woman part of the man runs gracefully toward the water
The man part walks toward the shore

At the nudist beach of the unconscious
the two parts go for a swim holding hands

The black sun rises on the horizon
The white sun blushes bright red

The woman and man make love till they're dizzy
Their bodies battle in the phosphorescent sand

And the firmament fills with meteors
traveling at the speed of light

Flora y fauna

En este pueblo viven los niños más viejos del mundo
Algunos tienen 200 años y otros 300

Pasean por las calles en monociclos descomunales
vestidos con ternos lilas y sombreros magritte

Vuelan por los aires en sus columpios de colores
Cazan luciérnagas con redecillas iridiscentes

Y andan entre las Rosas desfloradas
endulzándose la lengua con dorados néctares

En este pueblo las Violetas tienen caras
con mejillas sonrosadas y pupilas risueñas

Pero viven sus vidas completamente aterradas
de la decapitación por mano o tijera

Vengan niñitos a jugar con las Margaritas

Arránquenles los pétalos uno a uno
como si fueran patitas de moscas

Vengan niñitos a jugar a la ronda

Esta es la ronda de San Miguel
El que se ríe se va al cuartel
Uno dos y tres

Flora and Fauna

The oldest children in the world live in this town
Some are 200 years old and others 300

Dressed in lilac suits and Magritte hats
they go through the streets on enormous unicycles

They fly through the air on their colored swings
They chase lightning bugs with iridescent nets

And they walk among the deflowered Roses
sweetening their tongues with golden nectars

In this town the Violets have faces
with sunblushed cheeks and smiling eyes

But they live their lives completely terrified
a hand or scissors might lop their heads off

Come little children and play with the Daisies

Pluck out their petals one by one
as if they're little flies' feet

Come little children play ring-around

Ring around the rosy
Pocket full of posies
Ashes ashes
All fall down

John Lennon (1940–1980)

La vida comienza a los cuarenta
dijo John Lennon encendiendo las velas
en el comedor del edificio Dakota

La otra vida comienza ahora mismo
dijo la muerte apretando el gatillo
en la puerta del edificio Dakota

Porque después de esta muerte no hay otra
dijo la voz apagando las velas
y al que le venga el luto que se lo ponga

John Lennon (1940–1980)

Life begins at forty
John Lennon said lighting his birthday candles
in his dining room in the Dakota

The other life begins right now
death said squeezing the trigger
in the doorway of the Dakota

Because after this death there is no other
the voice said snuffing out the candles
so if mourning suits you wear it

Adán postrero

Sentado en un montón de escombros
espero a la mutante que será mi mujer

Mis pulmones son negros
y mi aliento huele a carbón

El viento dispersa árboles calcinados

Alguien me arranca una costilla
y la costilla se convierte en hollín

Hijo mío me dice
¿por qué me has abandonado?

Y se aleja pisando cenizas radiactivas

Last Adam

Sitting on a pile of debris
I wait for the mutant who'll be my wife

My lungs are black
and my breath smells like coal

Wind scatters the calcined trees

Someone rips out one of my ribs
and the rib turns to soot

My son he says
why have you abandoned me?

And backs away stepping on radioactive ash

Sigmund Freud bajo hipnosis

Mi vida psíquica es aún muy joven
y poco trabajadora

Un palacio sin luz
oculto en las profundidades del niño

Los órganos genitales son niños

Un pájaro baja y se posa
en los genitales de mi mujer

Esta visión me dejó grandemente confuso

Estoy tumbado por la tarde en el diván
casi vencido por la ensoñación

Veo una flor llamada lobelia

Entiendo que mi padre haya muerto
pero no entiendo por qué no viene a cenar

Vagaba por las calles para hacernos creer
que tenía un destino

Alguien trae mis ojos en un plato

La ensoñación prolonga la vida del niño
adentro del sujeto

La ensoñación es un arte involuntario

La vagina es un sendero blando y resbaladizo
por el que deben pasar los intérpretes

Los intérpretes hablan de ellos mismos
a propósito del sujeto

Sigmund Freud under Hypnosis

My psychic life's still very young
and not much of a worker

A lightless palace
hidden in the depths of the child

Genital organs are children

A bird descends and lights
on my wife's genitals

This image really confused me

Almost overcome by the dream
I spend the afternoon stretched out on the couch

I see a flower called a lobelia

I understand my father has died
but I don't understand why he doesn't come to supper

He wandered through the streets to make us believe
he had a destiny

Someone brings my eyes in on a plate

The dream prolongs the life of the child
inside the subject

Dreaming's an involuntary art

The vagina's a smooth and slippery path
analysts should pass through

Speaking about the subject
the analysts speak about themselves

El sujeto está tumbado por la tarde en el diván

Los intérpretes me ponen una careta de pájaro
y me la arrancan con toda la cara

Veo una flora llamada
la ensoñación de los intérpretes

Mi vida psíquica es ya muy vieja
pero muy trabajadora mamá

The subject spends the afternoon stretched out on the couch

The analysts put a birdmask on me
and rip it off with my whole face

I see a flower called
the analysts' dream

My psychic life's now very old
but a hard worker mama

Hipótesis celeste

L'amor che move il sole e l'altre stelle
—Dante, *Paradiso*, XXXIII

I

Las catedrales azules del cielo esplenden en la noche sin fin
y sus vitrales de colores dejan pasar la luz de otros mundos

Tu locura mi cielo brilla en la noche estelar

De tu frente sin orden
se alza un arcoiris que acaba en mi frente

Mi doncella de singular hermosura
duerme a la orilla de un arroyo celeste

De sus pies fluye el manantial de la vida

Recostado en la hierba espacial
yace un joven de risueñas formas y colores

Sobre su cabeza brillan lenguas de fuego

Su figura de ojos instantáneos
se eleva sin mancha a plena luz

Y convertido en lluvia de oro
dora el cuerpo de la hermosa doncella

Celestial Hypothesis

The love that moves the sun and the other stars
—Dante, *Paradiso*, XXXIII

I

The heavens' blue cathedrals shine in the endless night
and their stained glass lets in other worlds' light

Your madness heavenly one shines in the starry night

From your chaotic forehead
a rainbow rises and ends up on mine

My singularly beautiful maiden sleeps
on a celestial stream's bank

Life's spring flows from her feet

His colors and features smiling a young man lies
stretched out on astral grass

Tongues of fire flicker on his head

With instantaneous eyes his figure rises
stainless in the fullness of light

And changed into a golden rain
he gilds the beautiful maiden's body

II

Tu cuerpo parecía moverse hacia cualquier lugar del espacio

En medio de lo perecedero navega este astro sin luz

El cuerpo dio una vuelta completa alrededor de sus polos

Diste un gran círculo alrededor del sol
según el orden de los signos

Las estrellas fijas parecían mecernos
pero se mantenían inmóviles

La Tierra giraba contigo junto al aire circundante

Es preciso que el Cielo permanezca inmutable mi cielo
Es absolutamente necesario que no te muevas
ni un segundo-luz

El Sol real y el Sol irreal son uno y el mismo
me dijiste al oído

Retornan los astros a sus antiguas posiciones
y vuelven a alejarse querida

Repugna al orden del mundo que las cosas
estén fuera de su lugar natural
replicaste arreglándote el pelo

A los cuerpos simples
conviene un movimiento simple
murmuré penetrándote

En esto las esferas empezaron a rotar
en el aire vestido de hermosura y luz primera

Hace mucho tiempo que la Tierra
saltó en pedazos mi amor

II

Your body seemed to move randomly in outer space

This lightless star sails in the midst of what dies

Your body turned all the way around on its axis

You made a huge circle round the sun
following the order of the signs

The fixed stars seemed to rock us back and forth
but they were not moving

The Earth turned with you together with the circulating air

Heaven has to remain immutable heavenly one
It's absolutely necessary you not move
for even a light-second

Real Sun and unreal Sun are one and the same
you said in my ear

The stars return to their ancient positions
and go away again my dear

Fixing your hair you replied
If things are outside their natural places
the world's order is horrified

A simple movement is right
for simple bodies
I whispered as I entered you

And dressed with beauty and first light
the spheres began rotating in the air

It's been a long time since Earth
exploded my love

III

Ahora somos la luz
que se difunde en todas direcciones
y atraviesa los cuerpos opacos

Va fluyendo hacia el centro del universo
porque es la perfección de nuestros cuerpos

Cuando tu luz se multiplica un número infinito de veces
mi materia se extiende en dimensiones infinitas

Nuestro cuerpo es llamado firmamento mi amor

Así procedió la luz en el principio
A extender la materia arrastrándola con ella

Nuestro amor infinito
es más largo que otros infinitos

III

Now we're the light
that's scattered everywhere
and spans the dim bodies

Because it's the perfection of our bodies
it goes toward the center of the universe

When your light is multiplied infinitely
my matter is extended infinitely

Our body is called the firmament my love

In the beginning light happened that way
Extending matter by dragging it along

Our infinite love
is longer than other infinities

Sujeto en cuarto menguante

I

Mira la luna ahí afuera en lo alto. ¿Qué te parece? Me parece un poro. Es la luna llena. Llena de polen, digo. Me parece un poro y luego un punto negro. La luna es blanca, gallo. Blanco es el cielo y la luna un punto negro.

Subject in the Moon's Fourth Phase

I

Look at the moon up high out there. What does it look like to you? It looks to me like a pore. It's the full moon. Full of pollen, I say. It looks to me like a pore and then a blackhead. The moon's white, hotshot. The sky's white and the moon a blackhead.

II

Anoche oyeron gritar a alguien. Las brújulas me dijeron que se estaba haciendo tarde. ¿Tarde para qué?, les pregunté. Tarde no más, dijeron, riéndose de mí. Me fui caminando en cámara lenta. Oigan, brújulas, la risa abunda en boca de las histéricas. Somos almas en pena, dijeron. Sujeto, échate un vistazo hacia adentro y cuéntanos qué ves.

II

Last night they heard someone screaming. The witching ones told me it was getting late. Late for what? I asked them. Just late, they said, laughing at me. I was walking around in slow motion. Listen, witching ones, there's a lot of laughter in the mouths of hysterics. We're lost souls, they said. Subject, look inside yourself and tell us what you see.

III

Todas las cabezas iban bailando en procesión. Las verdes, adelante, cubiertas con ramas de tomillo. Las rojas, unos pasos atrás, pintadas con lápiz labial. Las amarillas, con cáscaras de papas pegadas en la frente. Me agarraron a peñascazos las muy cabronas. Me regaron con agua bendita. Me echaron alquitrán en el pelo. Pero yo seguí metido en la procesión, empapado, apestando a luna.

III

All the heads were dancing in a procession. The greens, farther on, covered with sprigs of thyme. The reds, several paces back, painted with lipstick. The yellows, with potato peels pasted on their foreheads. They stoned me the goddamn bitches. They sprinkled me with holy water. They poured tar on my hair. But I kept on, squeezed into the procession, soaked, smelling like the moon.

IV

Fue entonces cuando las lunas azules no pudieron más y se pusieron a gritar. Daban grandes aullidos de chanchos apaleados, chillidos de todos portes que ponían los pelos de punta. Cállense que sus bramidos me asustan más que mi cara, les dije. Mientras tanto las otras cabezas hacían preparativos para que me confundiera y avanzara por el camino errado y fuera a parar al fondo del precipicio.

IV

It happened when the blue moons couldn't take it anymore and started screaming. They let out great howls like pigs being beaten, all ranges of screams that stood your hair on end. Shut up or your roars'll frighten me more than my face, I told them. Meanwhile the other heads were preparing to confuse me and make me follow the wrong path and end up at the bottom of the cliff.

V

Aquí se detuvo el río de mi pensamiento. Se empozó y formó un charco. En este charco lleno mi tarrito con agua. Con esta agua mojo mi pan y lo chupo. Estoy afirmado contra una pared más blanca que mi pensamiento.

V

The river of my thought stopped here. It stagnated and formed a puddle. From this puddle I fill my can with water. With this water I wet my bread and suck it. I'm up against a wall that's whiter than my thoughts.

VI

Había un hilo perdido. Mi mamá me dijo: "Niño, tienes una hilacha en el suéter. Sácatela tú mismo, porque si no te va a traer mala suerte." Pisé la hilacha y se me pegó en la suela del zapato. Salí del cementerio y se me notaba la hilacha. Alguien me dijo: "Oiga, tiene una hilacha en el zapato." Y alguien más: "Es el hilo que se le había perdido."

VI

There was a loose thread. My mama told me: "Kid, you have a loose thread on your sweater. Pull it off or it'll bring you bad luck." I stepped on the loose thread and it stuck to my shoesole. I left the cemetery and the loose thread was visible. Someone said: "Listen, you have a loose thread on your shoe." And someone else: "It's the thread he lost."

VII

Había un hilo que deambulaba por todas partes buscando a su mamá. El hilo corría por la comisura de los labios. Hagámosle un homenaje al hilo perdido. Las personas depositan ofrendas florales en la tumba del hilo desconocido. Estás navegando sin timón por el sueño. Estás navegando a la deriva por el sueño, cantaron las brújulas.

VII

There was a thread that wandered around everywhere looking for its mama. The thread ran by the corners of the lips. Let's pay homage to the lost thread. People put floral offerings on the tomb of the unknown thread. You're sailing through a dream without a rudder. You're sailing adrift through a dream, the witching ones sang.

VIII

¿Corto la cara de la luna? No. Apriétala con las uñas para que le
salga el polen. Cuidado, oye, que me duele. Me saqué el punto
negro y ahora me está saliendo sangre. Lunático. Tú también.
Multiplícate por cero, loco.

VIII

Do I cut the face of the moon? No. Squeeze it with your finger-nails to get the pollen out. Careful, hey, that hurts. I got the black-head and now blood's coming out. Lunatic. You too. Multiply yourself by zero, nut.

estrellas fijas en un cielo blanco

fixed stars in a white sky

Estrellas fijas en un cielo blanco

Estrellas fijas en un cielo blanco
son los bellos sonetos pues no giran
en torno de orbe alguno ni han rotado
sus densas masas de catorce cifras

No reflejan la luz del sol tampoco
pero irradian su propia luz de adentro
Y en el albor parecen en reposo
o muertos cuyas tumbas son sus cuerpos

Y sin embargo las estrellas fijas
a veces bienhechoras o malignas
siempre de harta energía están cargadas

Y aunque hace miles de años extinguidas
su fulgor todavía nos alcanza
sea por vista o por astrología

Fixed Stars in a White Sky

Fixed stars in a white sky:
fine sonnets that do not turn
on any orbit, nor have their
fourteen dense masses spun

They don't reflect sun's light
but radiate their own light,
and in the whiteness seem at rest
or dead—their bodies their tombs

and whether they are benign
at times or malignant, fixed stars
always are energy-charged

And though they died millennia ago
still their brightness comes to us
by astrology or by sight

Lee Señor mis versos defectuosos

Lee Señor mis versos defectuosos
que quisieran salir pero no salen:
ya ves qué poco valen mis esfuerzos
y mis desdichas ay qué poco valen

Con tu ayuda saldrían universos
de palabras preñadas pero salen
débiles moribundos estos versos:
deja que el último suspiro exhalen

Ayúdame Señor: que no zozobre
en la mitad de este terceto pobre
mira estas ruinas: palpa su estructura

dónales lo que tengas que donarles:
y la vida que yo no supe darles
dásela tú Señor con tu lectura

Read My Defective Verses Lord

Read my defective verses Lord
They wanted light but found none:
you know the weakness of my strengths
the worthless value of my pain

If you would just help, worlds
pregnant with words would come
but my weak lines are moribund:
let them go on and die

Help me Lord: so I won't fall apart
in the middle of this poor tercet
look at these ruins: feel what they are

give what you have to give them:
and the life I couldn't give them
give them Lord as you read them

De cirios y de lirios

El lirio azul el lirio fucsia el lirio
de color colorado el lirio triste
con pétalos de cera se reviste
y va a la fiesta convertido en cirio

En cirio gris en cirio negro en cirio
de las aguas sin luz en cirio triste
que al llegar de la fiesta se desviste
y vuelve a ser en el jardín un lirio

O este espejo se está poniendo viejo
o lo que estoy mirando es un delirio
dice la flor hablándole al espejo

Adentro del azogue brota un cirio
y al tiempo que se enciende su reflejo
al fondo del jardín se apaga un lirio

Of Candles and Lilies

The blue lily the fuchsia lily
the blush-red lily the sad lily
dresses itself with petals of wax
and goes to the fest as a candle

A gray candle black candle candle
from lightless waters a sad candle
that on reaching the fest undresses
becoming a lily in the garden again

Either this mirror has gotten old
or what I'm looking at is crazy
says the flower to the mirror

A candle blooms in the mirror
and at the moment of its reflection
a lily's snuffed out in the garden

La Anunciación según
Fra Angelico

Siglo XV

La Virgen de rosado en una esquina
con manto azul: un pájaro se eleva
Un ángel de oro y rosa el cuerpo inclina
y le da con unción la buena nueva

Desde lo Alto un haz de luz divina
que en el extremo una paloma lleva
el vientre de la Virgen ilumina
cayendo oblicuamente

              adán y Eva
al destierro caminan entre flores

Con mano alada son iluminados
íconos de la Virgen en colores
azules rosas verdes y dorados

Preñó a la Virgen una luz divina
y a toda la pintura florentina

The Annunciation according to Fra Angelico

Fifteenth century

In a corner the Virgin dressed in pink
with a blue cape: a bird ascends
And in gold and pink an angel bends
to anoint her with the good news

And from on high a godly light
carries a dove at its farthest end
and slanting down shines on
the Virgin's womb

                        while in exile
Adam and Eve wander through flowers

Illuminated by a winged hand
the Virgin's icons receive
blues reds golds and greens

The godly light that brought the Virgin life
made Florentine painting breathe

Autorretrato hablado

Este retrato abrió la boca habló
y me dijo: ¿Qué tal? ¿Cómo se siente?
Me corrieron dos gotas por la frente
y el pelo casi se me encaneció

¿A quién le hablaba usted? pregunté yo
Le hablaba a mí me dijo sonriente
Y maliciosamente y de repente
el ojo izquierdo mío me guiñó

Este retrato abrió la boca oyó
mi propia voz diciéndose al oído:
Cosas de afuera quieren asustarme

Aquí mismo mi yo se ensimismó
y anda por el abismo tan perdido
que no he podido des-ensimismarme

Composite Drawing

Mouth opening this likeness spoke
and asked me: Hey! You okay?
Two drops ran down my forehead
and my hair almost turned gray

Who were you talking to? I asked
Smiling he said I was talking to me
Maliciously then and suddenly
my left eye winked at me

Mouth opening this likeness heard
my own voice telling its ear:
Things want to scare me out there

Here then my I got self-absorbed
and is now so lost in this abyss
I can't disabsorb myself

Soneto manco

Mi mano acecha: se repliega ufana
y salta encima de tu mano: no
vaya a ser que me pille al fin tu hermana
con la mano en la musa digo yo

Tu mano ajena me quitó la pena:
la mano de tu hermana me la dio
Desde la rabia de tu hermana buena
qué pesada su mano me cayó

Juego de hermanas juego de villanas
dijo la madre oliendo el gran secreto
mientras cortaba mis dos manos sanas

Porque yo me respeto no me arranco
y aquí estoy escribiendo este soneto
manco

Crippled Sonnet

Hidden now my hand fists up proud
and springs onto your hand: and may
your sister never catch me
with my hand in the muse I say

Though another's your hand is the one
that removed the pain your sister's hand
gave me—your good sister, her hand
fell hard she was so full of rage

Sister-games the games the trashy play
your mother cried sniffing our big secret out
as she whacked off my two good hands

Because I respect myself I'm not
hotfooting off: I'm here writing this sonnet
that's crippled

¿Por qué escribe usted?

Porque el fantasma porque ayer porque hoy
porque mañana porque sí porque no
Porque el principio porque la bestia porque el fin
porque la bomba porque el medio porque el jardín

Porque góngora porque la tierra porque el sol
porque san juan porque la luna porque rimbaud
Porque el claro porque la sangre porque el papel
porque la carne porque la tinta porque la piel

Porque la noche porque me odio porque la luz
porque el infierno porque el cielo porque tú
Porque casi porque nada porque la sed
porque el amor porque el grito porque no sé

Porque la muerte porque apenas porque más
porque algún día porque todos porque quizás

Why Do You Write?

Because yesterday because today because the ghost
because tomorrow because yes because no
Because the beginning because the beast because the end
because the bomb because the center because the garden

Because góngora because the earth because the sun
because rimbaud because the moon because saint john
Because the bright because blood because paper
because flesh because skin because color

Because hell because heaven because night
because I hate myself because you because light
Because nothing because thirst because almost
because love because clamor because I don't know

Because death because more because scarcely
because someday because all because maybe

A una lavandera de Santiago

Mi prima que vivía de su artesa
se me murió de muerte repentina:
le partieron de un golpe la cabeza
con la culata de una carabina

Desde el abismo de su cráneo abierto
suben gritos y cantos fraternales:
entran en cada vivo en cada muerto
y enmudecen las músicas marciales

La ropa sucia no se lava en casa
cuando la manchan sangres tan enormes
que van de lavatorio en lavatorio

Un regimiento de manchados pasa:
y no podrá limpiar sus uniformes
ni el mismo purgador del Purgatorio

To a Santiago Washerwoman

My cousin who lived off her tubs
suddenly died on me:
one blow from a rifle butt
and her head opened up

Out of her splayed skull's pit
screams and fraternal songs rise:
entering each life and each death
they mute the martial tunes

When stains of blood are so huge
they flow from basin to basin
dirty clothes aren't washed at home

A regiment of stained men passes:
so dirty even Purgatory's purger
could never clean their uniforms

Visiones de San Narciso

Un Cristo bizantino he recortado
desde un libro de láminas muy viejo
y luego con saliva lo he pegado
junto a mi cara encima del espejo

Me mira el Cristo: frunce el entrecejo
y de golpe me siento avergonzado
Quiero alejarme pero no me alejo:
en la cruz del espejo estoy clavado

Miro al Cristo con ojos suplicantes
y el cristal me retorna unas sonrisas
que me recuerdan trágicos instantes

Lo saco del azogue: lo devuelvo
a su cruz de papel: y cuando vuelvo
el centro del espejo se hace trizas

Visions of Saint Narcissus

I cut a Byzantine Christ
out of an old art book
then with spit stuck it above
the mirror near my face

His brow wrinkling, the Christ looks
at me: I'm suddenly ashamed
I want to withdraw but I can't:
I'm nailed to the mirror's cross

Eyes supplicant I look at the Christ
and the pane sends back smiles
then memories of tragedies rise

I peel him off the glass: return him
to his paper cross: but when I turn back
the mirror's center shatters

Descendiente de cuervo o gallinazo

Tanta esterilidad llevo en mi pluma
que me pluma ni vuela ni aletea:
se adormece en mi mano: cabecea
y espera que la tinta se consuma

Yo pensé que mi pluma era de gallo
que alguna vez fue gallo de pelea
y ahora mal plumífero me hallo
porque mi pluma sólo cacarea

Todo es volátil: menos el plumífero
que en su carne de pájaro mamífero
acarrea mi pluma desdichada

Todo en la muerte es humareda: acaso
descendiente de cuervo o gallinazo
allí me haré volátil: humo y nada

A Crow's or Buzzard's Get

The pen I carry is so barren
it neither flies nor flutters: just drifts
asleep in my hand: head ajerk
waiting for its ink to dry

I thought my pen was real cocky
once even fighting cock cocky
but now I find myself poorly penned
because my pen just goes *cluck-cluck*

Everything shifts: except the pen-
bearer carrying my sorry pen
about in his mammalian birdflesh

Whether you're crow's or buzzard's get
everything's smoky in death:
there I'll really shift shapes: whiff then *poof!*

Tríptico

I. Adán sentado con las manos en la barbilla

Abrí las siete puertas del deseo
y no hallé adentro cosa deseable
y he buscado que hable lo inefable
pero se expresa a puro balbuceo

Mi pensamiento entonces da un rodeo
de hilo negro enredado interminable
que no quiere pensar en lo más feo
y termina pensando lo impensable

Mi pensamiento sucio se menea
prende fuego a los árboles: jadea
y embarazado de sí mismo grita

Como queriendo darse a luz husmea:
asoma la cabeza: balbucea
y una estatua de sal lo decapita

Triptych

I. Adam Sitting, Chin in Hand

I opened the seven doors of desire
and discovered I wanted nothing there:
I've sought the speech of the ineffable
but its sounds are incomprehensible

And now my thoughts take a turn
into an endless black and tangled line
that hates to think about wretched things
and ends up thinking unthinkable things

Dirty my thought line goes here then there
and sets the trees on fire: it gasps for air
and is pregnant now with its own uproar

As if trying to birth itself it noses out
its head appears bobbing babbling about
then a statue made of salt unheads it

II. Adán recuerda la fallida destrucción del árbol de la ciencia

Árbol de nuestro amor a cuya lumbre
saboreamos los frutos prohibidos
hasta que amenazados por la herrumbre
huimos del jardín enmohecidos

Río de este vergel en cuya orilla
nos mojamos los pies ardiendo juntos
y despertamos de esa maravilla
vivos pero vestidos de difuntos

Caminamos tomados de la mano
y el gran río cruzamos vengativos
para incendiar los bosques tentadores

Y al calcinarse el último manzano
nuestros límpidos cuerpos radiactivos
se cubrieron de frutas y de flores

II. Adam Remembers the Vain Attempt to Destroy the Tree of Knowledge

Tree of our love in whose glow
we savored forbidden fruit
till threatened by corrosion
we fled the garden corrupted

River of this orchard from whose bank
we two wet our burning feet
and from that wonder awoke
alive but dressed like the dead

Hand in hand we walked and out
for revenge crossed the great river
to set the tempter woods on fire

And the last apple tree turning to ashes
our radioactive bodies, naked and pure,
were covered with fruit and with flowers

III. La expulsión del Paraíso

Tu lecho es el jardín de las delicias
encarnas en tu cuerpo a las tres gracias
con tus flores y frutas me acaricias
y de mi ser más íntimo me vacias

Después cuando mis ramas quedan lacias
en otros ritos del placer me inicias:
con tus lenguas de fuego me suplicias
y somos el jardín de las desgracias

Rodamos por oscuros precipicios
y oficiamos diabólicos oficios
en dormitorios de incendiadas camas

Y cuando huimos de esos maleficios
nos espera en la puerta de los vicios
un ser alado con un lirio en llamas

III. Expulsion from Paradise

Your bed, the garden of delights
your body, three graces flesht
your fruits and flowers caressing me,
intimately you empty me

When my limbs lie limp, you guide me
into other delightful rites:
your flaming tongues entreating me,
we are the garden of shameful needs

Roaming the edges of dark heights
we celebrate demonic rites
in bedrooms whose beds are on fire

And when we flee those wicked spells
a winged being with lily afire
waits for us at the door of desire

Reloj de arena

Desdichado lector tuya es la mano
que puso en marcha este reloj de arena:
las sílabas ya caen grano a grano
allá abajo palpita tu condena

Estas líneas que miras ahora mismo
son columnas de arena vertical:
vas con ellas fluyendo hacia el abismo
vas goteando hacia el fondo del cristal

Ay cómo entre los versos te deslizas
Mira cuán bajo has descendido ya
De peldaño en peldaño viento pisas:
casi vacío el otro vaso está

Se te acaba la arena: no hay demora
Despídete lector: llegó tu hora

Hourglass

It's your hand, poor reader
that set this hourglass going:
grain by grain the syllables fall,
your fate's stirring down there

And these lines you're looking at
are vertical sand columns:
dropping with them toward crystal's end
you flow toward the abyss with them

See how you slip in between lines
See how much lower you've gotten
Step by step you walk on wind:
the upper bulb's almost empty

Your sand's gone: no way to stop
Reader say bye-bye: nothing up top

otros poemas

other poems

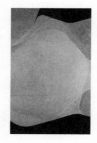

Un ahogado pensativo
a veces desciende

Septiembre de 1973

Hay un muerto flotando en este río
y hay otro muerto más flotando aquí

Esta es la hora en que los grandes símbolos
huyen despavoridos: mira el agua

hay otro muerto más flotando aquí

Alguien corre gritando un nombre en llamas
que sube a tientas y aletea y cae
dando vueltas e ilumina la noche

hay otro muerto más flotando aquí

Caudaloso de cuerpos pasa el río
Almas amoratadas hasta el hueso
vituperadas hasta al desperdicio

hay otro muerto más flotando aquí

Duerme flotación pálida desciende
a descansar: la luna jorobada
llena el aire de plata leporina

Tomados de la mano van los muertos
Caminando en silencio sobre el agua

A Pensive Drowned Man
Sometimes Drifts

September 1973

There's a corpse floating on this river
and still another corpse floating by

Now's the time when great symbols
flee terrified: look at the water

still another corpse floating by

Someone runs screaming a name in flames
that flailing rises flutters and falls
turning and lights up the night

still another corpse floating by

A horde of bodies on the river:
souls bruised down to bone
abused until they're junk

still another corpse floating by

Sleep pale flotsam: drift down
to rest: the humpbacked moon fills
the harelike silver air

Holding hands the corpses go:
walking on the water in silence

Fábula del lenocinio

Ahorcaron a una prostituta
con volutas
de humo negro triste y sospechoso

Cuatro besos de cera
eran las velas
con que adornaban todos
el ataúd
Unos lloraban vino
otros bebían
charcos de virgen muerta
a su salud

Cuelga en la cabecera
como una pierna
cuelga como campana
ya sin sonido
cuelga como un lamento
desvanecido
cuelga como una colcha
tapando lirios
Todo cuelga esta noche
cuelga la muerte
cuelga la prostituta
de la humareda

Ahorcaron a una prostituta
con volutas
de humo negro triste y sospechoso
y está en silencio colgando
                              para allá
para acá
                    para allá
          y para acá

Whorehouse Lore

They strung up a prostitute
with swirls
of sad black suspicious smoke

Four wax kisses
were the candles
they all adorned
the coffin with
Some cried wine
others drank
dead virgin puddles
to her health

She hangs from the headboard
like a leg
she hangs like a bell
already mute
she hangs like a lament
vanished
she hangs like a bedspread
covering lilies
Tonight everything hangs
death hangs
the prostitute hangs
from the smoke cloud

They strung up a prostitute
with swirls
of sad black suspicious smoke
and hanging in silence she sways

       that way
this way

     that way
   and this way

Letanía para un poeta difunto

Ahora o un primero de noviembre
me recuerdo de tu infinita muerte

de tu mortaja pálido arcoiris
tejido por las manos de la muerte

de la hierba que invade tus ojeras
como pestañas puestas por la muerte

de las cavernas de tu pensamiento
pintarrajeadas negras por la muerte

de tus palabras nunca entumecidas
derramándose fuera de la muerte

de tu resurrección en mi marea
como surgen las almas de la muerte

las verdaderas almas de la muerte
las poéticas almas de la muerte

Litany for a Dead Poet

Now or on a November first
I remember your infinite death

your shroud a pale rainbow
woven by the hands of death

grass invading your eyesockets
like eyelashes placed by death

the caverns of your thoughts
smeared black by death

your never-numb words
spilling out beyond death

your resurrection in my tide
like souls rising from death

true souls rising from death
poetic souls rising from death

Restricción de los
desplazamientos nocturnos

O el animal super-chico cuyo cuerpo crece o decrece
de izquierda a derecha:

o el cazador moviéndose hacia la bestezuela
de derecha a izquierda:

o la línea que se borra o se marca en el pizarrón
de izquierda a derecha:

o el borrador deslizándose hacia el punto blanco
de derecha a izquierda:

o el cazador o el borrador como únicos sobrevivientes
en esta hoja:
o esta hoja que arrugo o que tiro en el papelero:

o ese algo que avanza hacia mí por el cuarto sin ruido

de abajo arriba: de arriba abajo:
de izquierda a derecha o de derecha a izquierda:

y me arruga y me tira en el papelero

Restriction of
Nocturnal Movements

Or the super-little animal whose body increases or decreases
from left to right:

or the hunter moving toward the little beast
from right to left:

or the line that's erased or drawn on the blackboard
from left to right:

or the eraser gliding toward the white point
from right to left:

or the hunter or the eraser as sole survivors
on this page:
or this page I wad up and toss in the wastebasket:

or this thing noiselessly moving through the room toward me

upward: downward:
left to right or right to left:

wadding me up, tossing me in the wastebasket

Soy una piedra lanzada de canto

Muerte escondida en los arrabales del silencio
en los sutiles pliegues de las sombras
¿soy el lanzado como una piedra por la mano de Dios
en el agua de la existencia?
¿soy el que en ondas circulares irá creciendo
hasta desbordarse en el vacío sin fin?

Porque ahora
como una tangente en agonía
toqué el acuoso círculo de las ondas despeñables
y lleno de pavor
como quien ve resucitar a sus muertos olvidados
sentí hambre de espacio y sed de cielo

Se romperá el espejo de mi vigilia
y no reflejará mis carnes en la florida tierra
Pero hay que morirse con las uñas largas
para poder cogerse del recuerdo

I'm a Skipping-Stone

Death hidden in the outskirts of silence
in the subtle creases of shadows
am I the one God's hand tossed like a rock
into the water of existence?
am I the one who'll grow in circular waves
till I spill into the endless void?

Because now
like a tangent in its last throes
I touched the watery circle of the crashing waves
and full of fear
like someone who sees his forgotten dead reviving
I felt hungry for space and thirsty for sky

My vigil's mirror will break
and won't reflect my flesh on the flowering earth
But if you're going to grab memory
you have to die with long fingernails

Año viejo 1973

Se terminó este año cabrón. Se fue a la cresta.
Se fue completamente a pique: capotó.
Con sus terrores y llantos y entierros a cuestas
y los cuatro jinetes del apocalipsis.

Ahora está sonando la sirena. Y ahora mismo
estallan los fuegos artificiales. Y ahora
comienzan los abrazos. "A año muerto
año puesto" me decías con una copa en la mano
corriéndote las lágrimas. "Que seas feliz."

Se terminó este año cabrón. Se fue a la cresta.

Old Year 1973

This goddamn year's over. Everything hit the fan.
Went over the edge and all to hell.
With its terrors and tears and burial loads
and the four horsemen of the apocalypse.

The siren's blowing now. And now
fireworks are going off. And now
embraces begin. "To the dead year
the done year" you told me tears flowing
drink in hand. "Happy New Year."

This goddamn year's over. Everything hit the fan.

The year of the military coup in Chile: the rise of Augusto Pinochet and the fall of Salvador Allende.—TRANSLATOR

Hotel de las nostalgias

Música de Elvis Presley

Nosotros
los adolescentes de los años 50

los del jopo en la frente
y el pucho en la comisura

los bailarines de rock and roll
al compás del reloj

los jóvenes coléricos
maníacos discomaníacos

dónde estamos ahora
que la vida es de minutos nada más

asilados en qué Embajada
en qué país desterrados

enterrados
en qué cementerio clandestino

Porque no somos nada
sino perros sabuesos

Nada
sino perros

Heartbreak Hotel

Elvis Presley's music

We
the teenagers of the 50s

the ones with dangling forelocks
and cigarette butts hanging off our lipcorners

rock and roll dancers
rocking round the clock

angry young men
maniac recordmaniacs

where are we now
that life's but a matter of minutes

refugees in what Embassy
exiled in what country

buried
in what clandestine cemetery

'Cause we ain't nothing
but hound dogs

Nothing
but dogs